FROM DIS'S WAGGON

—O Proserpina!
For the flowers now that frighted thou lett'st fall
From Dis's Waggon.   "A Winter's Tale"

A Sentimental Survey of a Poets' Corner
The Shakespeare Garden of Cleveland
By Leo Weidenthal

1926--- THE WEIDENTHAL COMPANY---CLEVELAND

The Central Path Bordered by Evergreen and Eglantine

*To the Discoverers of the Poets' Corner that
hugs the Hearthstone of Civilization's House*

FROM DIS'S WAGGON

A Sentimental Survey of a Poets' Corner---
The Shakespeare Garden of Cleveland

AUTHOR'S PREFACE

Gardens of the general type described in the following pages have become a recognized part of park landscaping. Of standard works dealing with Elizabethan Gardens in a comprehensive and technically adequate manner, there is now a formidable array.

No effort has been made in this volume to cover that ground. Emphasis has been laid, instead, upon those features which are distinctive and unique in the setting and marking of the Poets' Garden of Cleveland. Its treasured mementos, including trees and shrubs planted by eminent actors, poets and playwrights during their visits to Cleveland, and incidents of these little jaunts, are described.

In conclusion, there is narrated a bit of Cleveland's theatrical history during a period in the life of the American stage when Shakespeare was serving as the mainstay in stock and traveling company repertoire.

This book appears at a time when the Poets' Corner of Cleveland, despite its advancing years, is still in the development stage and when plans for its extension and improvement are in the making.

Partial explanation may be found in this, for some obvious but unavoidable awkwardness in arrangement.

For other shortcomings and failings not so easily brushed aside, the reader's indulgence is respectfully sought. It is the hope of the author that the chief purpose of this work, namely, the recording of the beginnings and early phases of a fine and worthy civic enterprise, may prove an influence for generously inclusive condonation.

September, 1926.

ILLUSTRATIONS

ACKNOWLEDGMENTS

Illustrations showing Julia Marlowe and E. H. Sothern, Bialik and the "Midsummer Night's Dream" production are reproduced from photographs by Andrew L. Kraffert, Plain Dealer staff photographer.

Illustrations showing Ethel Barrymore at the Outdoor Theater are from photographs by L. Van Oeyen, N. E. A. Service, Inc.

General views of the Garden are from photographs by David L. and William Sperling.

Portraits of John A. Ellsler, Effie Ellsler and Clara Morris are from photographs that formed a part of the collection of the late Maurice Weidenthal.

Portrait of Marie Leah Bruot is by the Chircosta Studio.

Academy of Music playbill illustration is a reproduction of a program in the collection of William R. Rose.

Plan of Shakespeare Garden furnished through courtesy of Raymond F. Persche, City Forester.

CONTENTS

FROM DIS'S WAGGON

EARTH-BORNE trailing clouds of glory are the garden playgrounds of a poet's fancy; garlands from Dis's Waggon, well worth the weaving and wearing. A modern city, lingering but a little, to gather poor Proserpina's scattered treasures, merits no rebuke, for in that primrose path of dalliance rests refutation of the oft repeated charge of utter worldliness.

One such sentimental journey forms the thesis of this volume. Fragile, indeed. Such stuff, in very truth, as dreams are made on.

The Poets' Corner nestling in the heart of a great city's park system is, of necessity, a thing apart from the trappings and the suits of urban convention.

It is a byway mood; a bit of tenderness, shyly revealed; a whispered avowal of faith and confidence.

Let skeptics sneer. The city believes. Year after year, tiny roses from a garden in far off Verona, blossom and fade and bloom again in the Poets' Corner of Cleveland as an attestation of that faith. The Lady Juliet lived and loved and died, and there's an end on 't.

If there are barriers twixt city planning and city dreaming, Cleveland has easily o'erleaped them in this adventure.

To chronicle such a flight, there is but little need for imagery or charm. The goal's the thing.

There every tree and flower chants with the Choir Invisible "whose music is the gladness of the world" and in its higher resonance its light and inspiration.

For, after all, such stuff as poet-prophet dreams are made on pervades the great realities that history extols.

Something of this, something far nobler than the leaf-fringed legend of a Grecian urn, sounds from this sylvan historian.

Congealed happiness spreads no frozen grimace here. Here are no Pollyanna boughs that cannot shed their leaves

"Nor ever bid the spring adieu."

Proserpina's blossoms live but in succession. Were they mere painted images, the city, Perdita-like, would scorn to put the dibble in earth to set one slip of them.

Living, glowing, mortal children of earth and air and sunlight and rain and wind and storm—these are the poet's message bearers.

Dis's Waggon knows no others.

In our Poets' Corner may no others find tenancy.

IN SHAKESPEARE'S GARDEN

■OT as a weak witness of a towering name, but rather as a tangible expression of the loveliness which inspired a master poet's loftiest flights, has the Shakespeare Garden assumed its place in the sun. To carry the institution safely beyond the pervue of Milton's withering denunciation of Shakespeare memorials it is needful that this distinction be set forth with alacrity and force.

To summon on every hand the beauty that was dear to Shakespeare is to make available the great source book whose pages were conned by him from shining-faced school boy days by murmuring Avon, to the blazing noon-tide of Verona, and

At the Upper Garden Entrance

from Romeo to Prospero and twilight in the quiet arbors of New Place.

Holinshed was not his major mentor. The mighty chronicles of Mother Nature proved ample inspiration. From these he gleaned the formulae for luminous pigments that glow undimmed today upon his immortal canvasses—Titania's violet bank, Capulet's orchard, the glades of Arden, Perdita's marigold beds, the cypress bordered avenue to Portia's Belmont villa and all the rest that live in his great garden gallery.

Adaptable, companionable, self-forgetting to a fault, Shakespeare's Garden is a creation of a myriad garbs and moods. It romps with the daisies of the bordering fields, smiles at the tribbing fairies of Windsor green, sighs with Mariana of the moated grange and casts loving eyes upon the neighboring greenwood shade, eager to wander hand in hand with peripatetic Birnam or to share hostship with Arden; ready if need be to grow a clock and mantelpiece as well, should Rosalind bid the time o' the day.

Dreams of mute, inglorious Shakespeares stirred to melodic utterance in days to come may add some zest to Shakespeare Garden planning and planting. But poet-baiting is not the only spur. The older laurels are still fresh and green.

Shakespeare's beacon flame still lights the path ahead.

THE CLEVELAND GARDEN

CLEVELAND'S SHAKESPEARE GARDEN came into being on the tercentenary of the poet's death. Mid the grimmest struggle that ever darkened the face of the globe there were myriads, even in lands engaged in deadly warfare, who remembered on April 23, 1916, that 300 years before, the mighty creator of Lear, Hamlet and Macbeth broke his staff, drowned his book and laid him down in his last sleep.

A hillside east of the valley of Doan brook in Rockefeller Parkway and midway between St. Clair and Superior avenues had been selected by the City as the site for the Garden that was to bear the Shakespeare name.

The Shakespeare Mulberry

Closely planted hedges of arbor vitae were used in marking its general outlines. A wide central walk and long outer paths all converging at the easterly end of the slope, defined the Elizabethan plot as laid out under the direction of City Forester John Boddy.

In beds bordered by yew were planted the English garden favorites which Shakespeare knew and loved. Hawthorn, some clipped and some in unshorn loveliness, soon loomed amid the low clusters of shrubs and flowers. Of the latter, the selection was made to form an unending pageant for the garden year, from daffodils "that come before the swallows dare" to the more brilliant-hued flowers of late summer and fall. Of violets, the flower-de-luce, daisies, pansies and columbines, there was a plenteous host.

American Hawthorn Near Entrance Gate

Many others, beloved by the Avon bard and by all minstrels, time out of mind, were also accorded space in appropriate nooks and corners. Barberry hedges which had lined the central path when the plot served as a city tree nursery in pre-Shakespeare Garden days, were replaced by more appropriate hedges of eglantine with its all-pervading fragrance. Behind these were set two sentinel rows of tapering evergreen.

Flanking the conventional sections of the Garden, to the north and south, two groves were laid out, the southerly cluster consisting of descendants of one of the last two remaining trees of the ancient Scottish wood that rose against a most notorious usurper and tyrant a thousand years ago. These baby sycamore maples, today begin to flaunt the "leavy screens" that formed so effective a camouflage for the army of Malcolm in its march upon Macbeth.

Thus has Birnam Wood come to the Shakespeare Garden of Cleveland.

With the maple seedlings, Scotland, in 1916, sent a limb hewn from an old oak, the other remnant of majestic Birnam. This was made into a chair of an old English pattern.

A wing of the Garden extends into Birnam. In the center of this, each summer, is set out a bed of "Juliet" roses grown from cuttings sent to the city in 1916 by the Mayor of Verona. They are from the tomb of the Capulets.

Erudite scholars question the authenticity of the tomb. Some have even ventured to extend their doubtings to the historicity of the pair of star-crossed lovers whose names form the title of the sweetest of all tragedies.

Cleveland stands with the poet.

Balancing the southerly wing is a garden room or extension which forms a lovely background for a sun dial, a gift of Robert B. Mantell,

Tomb of Capulets—Verona

which has adorned the Garden for many years. The presentation was made by the distinguished actor, from the stage of a Cleveland theater.

A garden bust of Shakespeare was placed in the semi-circular converging point of the Garden paths in the fall of 1916. The central path, now paved with flagstone, and walled by evergreen and eglantine, forms a picturesque approach to this sculptural memorial which is the work of Joseph C. Motto and Stephen A. Rebeck.

The bust was formally dedicated on October 21, 1916. Alex Bernstein, director of public service, William J. Raddatz and Judge Willis Vickery were speakers.

In 1916 the city through the efforts of the late Sir Sidney Lee, Shakespeare's greatest biographer and for years a leading spirit in the preservation and beautification of historic sites at Stratford. received a cutting of the mulberry planted by the poet himself in his New Place grounds more than 300 years ago. This scion of a famous sire, in 1926 was placed in a prominent position, near the bust. In that year, on the anniversary of the poet's birth and death, the circular garden bench now enclosing the tree was dedicated. The Shakespeare Society was the donor of the bench, and the Federation of Women's Clubs directed the birthday observance.

Bruot Memorial Gate—Entrance to Theater

But all of this was still to come when the city in 1916, the tercentenary year, made ready for its inaugural planting ceremony. The event was set for April 14 and the guests of honor and principals were those two luminaries of the Shakespeare firmament, Julia Marlowe and E. H. Sothern.

Mrs. Sothern was in temporary retirement from the stage at the time, but was accompanying Mr. Sothern on his tour. The city's invitation to participate in the Shakespeare Garden planting was tendered to both.

The exercises took place on the upper Boulevard near the Garden entrance. There were addresses by city officials, one of whom, Floyd E. Waite, earnestly and eloquently importuned the guests to reconsider their then but recently announced decision to move to England, expressing the belief that the Mayor "would give them a large slice of this park if they would only consent to live in Cleveland."

Julia Marlowe Planting Marlowe Elm

E. H. Sothern and Julia Marlowe at Garden Planting Ceremony

Harry L. Davis, then Mayor of Cleveland, and later Governor of Ohio, seconded the plea and Mr. Sothern in a brief response gravely voiced his and Mrs. Sothern's deep appreciation.

An orchestra played Shakespeare music. The Normal Glee Club rendered Shakespeare choral selections and a most fitting touch was lent to the old English character of the program by the attendance of a group of Glenville High School pupils, in the garb that was modish in Shakespeare's day.   These youthful Eliza-bethans aided in escorting Mr. Sothern and Miss Marlowe to the Garden entrance to plant the two American elms, which were to stand guard at the gateway.

Miss Marlowe's contribution to the day's program was the reading of Perdita's flower greeting, from "Winter's Tale."

No part of Shakespeare, it may be argued with some force, gives greater point to Bernard Shaw's contention that the Bard of Avon dallied with words that linger in the memory like the refrain of a lovely song:

—"Sir, the year growing ancient,
Nor yet on summer's death, nor on the birth
Of trembling winter, the fairest flowers o' the season
Are our carnations and streaked gillyvors."

A myriad wistful Marlowe Juliets, Rosalinds and Violas poured the rich cadence of their golden eloquence into the wel-come:

—"O Proserpina!
For the flowers now that frighted thou lett'st fall
From Dis's waggon! daffodils,
That come before the swallow dares, and take
The winds of March with beauty; violets dim,
But sweeter than the lids of Juno's eyes
Or Cytherea's breath; pale primroses,
That die unmarried, ere they can behold
Bright Phoebus in his strength, a malady
Most incident to maids; bold oxlips and
The crown-imperial; lilies of all kinds,
The flower-de-luce being one. O! these I lack
To make you garlands of, and my sweet friend,
To strew him o'er and o'er."

Miss Marlowe's rendition of this glorious "word-music" was followed by her reading of a Shakespeare Sonnet, the Fifty-fourth, and this with verses from the "Star Spangled Banner." At the close of the program the renowned actress led the entire gathering in the singing of the National Anthem.

Shakespeare Bust and Fountain—Converging Point of All the Garden Pathways

MEMENTOS

HROUGH the passing years, many noted actors, poets, novelists, playwrights and theatrical producers visited the Shakespeare Garden. Trees inscribed with their names stand as living memorials of these occasions.

In many instances formal programs marked the tree planting events. In other cases, the visits were informal and quite unmarked by any set ceremonies.

Available tree areas in the immediate vicinity of the bust rapidly dwindled and the city, for this reason, in later years became inclined to the policy of setting aside the outer spaces for planting.

Shakespeare Gardens have come into being since the more elaborate development of New Place grounds at Stratford, in many parts of the world, but in Cleveland there was an early effort to individualize the Poets' Grounds by featuring mementos of the

Effie Ellsler Among the Home Folks

reception of famous guests.   This custom has won added interest for the Garden.

The special plantings, from Old World sections identified with Shakespeare's immortal plays, have also been a distinguishing feature of the Cleveland Garden memorial.

The willows, growing near the dais which supports the fountain and bust, were planted by William Faversham and Daniel Frohman.   Mr. Frohman visited the Garden while in Cleveland in 1919 planning an Actors' Fund benefit day.

William Faversham

Close to the Frohman willow is an oak planted by William Butler Yeats, the Irish poet who, on the occasion of his visit, recited one of his own poems.   The poet was introduced by William R. Rose, associate editor of the Plain Dealer, with an expression of the earnest hope that the Yeats oak would grow so strong and mighty that fays and elves would come to love it and would steal out at the witching hour to dance around it in the moonlight.

Near the Yeats oak grows an oak planted in 1916 by Phyllis Neilson Terry, daughter of Fred Terry and niece of the immortal Ellen.

In the same section Vachel Lindsay, American poet, planted a poplar some years later and in honor of the occasion recited an original poetical tribute to the Bard of Avon.

In 1919, Edwin Markham and Mrs. Aline Kilmer, widow of the soldier poet, Joyce Kilmer, visited the Garden on the same day.   Both had been invited to the city to address organizations and the city had seized this opportunity to ask both to plant trees.   City Forester Harry C. Hyatt, during the ceremony, offered the poet a hoe, but Mr. Markham observed that through his "Man With a Hoe" he had done all he could do for that implement and was at that moment in need of a spade for the tree planting.   A photographer near by snapped the poet as he stood shovel in hand.   The rejected hoe lay at his feet as the picture was taken, mute evidence of the poet's earnest zeal for the newer task in hand.

Mr. Markham, filled with enthusiasm, led the way as the party inspected the Garden, and told of his tree-caring experiences in his orchard in Southern California years before.   Mr. Markham was a speaker at Florence Harkness Memorial Chapel during his visit in Cleveland.

Phyllis Neilson Terry

Mrs. Kilmer was in Cleveland under the auspices of the Ursuline Convent A l u m n i Association. Following the planting, t h e widow of the young poet, herself a gifted poet, addressed the Women's City Club.

A joint visit was also paid by Otis Skinner, renowned actor, and Stephen A. Leacock, humorist. Both planted trees near the section that has since become Birnam Wood. Hugh Walpole also planted a tree in honor of the poet.

David Belasco was a visitor at the Garden in 1916.   The wish voiced by him that the two junipers which he planted would live as long and keep as green as the memory of the man honored by the city with the Garden tribute, has not been fulfilled.   The two Belasco junipers did not long survive.   A brief existence, too, was that of the first elm planted by Mr. Sothern, but another elm was planted by him on a subsequent visit to the city.   This tree was planted a year after the dedication ceremony.   A few other trees linked with the visits of noted persons have passed away, but in the main, the mortality rate has not been high.

To David Belasco, the visit at the Shakespeare Garden brought

Edwin Markham and Aline Kilmer at the Garden—City Forester Hyatt, Center

recollections of his association with the plays of the Bard and their mightiest interpreters.

It was little David Belasco, aged eleven, who played the Duke of York to the Richard of the son of Edmund Kean. This was in the year 1864 when Charles Kean was engaged in a farewell tour of the world. At twenty-one, David Belasco, on the stage of the California Theater, San Francisco, danced the minuet with the Juliet of lovely Adelaide Neilson in the ballroom of the Capulets. A few years later, as stage manager of the Baldwin, it was young Belasco who aided Adelaide Neilson in her descent from the balcony after her last reading of Shakespeare's

unforgettable lines.   Adelaide Neilson appeared as Juliet and Rosalind at the Academy of Music in Cleveland in the spring of 1873.
J. Newton Gotthold was her leading man, and other parts in her
presentations were taken by members of the Ellsler company.

It was the Belasco of those years who dreamed of becoming
the greatest Hamlet, the greatest Iago of the age.   Just twenty-
five years prior to his visit at the Shakespeare Garden, Belasco had
introduced to Cleveland a rising young star, who had made her
stage debut under his direction but a few weeks before in "The
Ugly Duckling." Cleveland was not unknown to Mrs. Leslie Car-
ter, afterwards to rise to the topmost round of theatrical fame in
"Du Barry" and "Zaza." In her girlhood, as little Caroline
Dudley, she had lived in Cleveland and had attended old Rock-
well School, now in the heart of the city's business district.

The late George Gibbs Mansfield, only child of the eminent
actor, Richard Mansfield, was a visitor in Cleveland shortly
before his death in the Service, and accepted an invitation to plant
a tree in the Shakespeare Garden as a memorial to his father, whose
Richard III, Shylock and Brutus are described by critics of
some decades ago as among the outstanding Shakespeare interpre-
tations of the age.   Because of violently inclement weather on the
day named for the planting, city officials in charge did not com-
plete arrangements for the ceremony.   Afterwards it was learned

Chaim Nachman Bialik Honored by City

Belasco Planting a Juniper in Shakespeare Garden—With him are his Secretary
and Floyd E. Waite and Philmore J. Haber, City Department Secretaries

with great regret that young Mr. Mansfield had hoped to proceed with the planting and had tried, unsuccessfully, to communicate with those in charge.

Effie Ellsler, visiting her girlhood home and the city of her earliest stage triumphs, was invited by city officials to be the principal in a tree planting ceremony. William R. Rose again acted as master of ceremonies on this occasion. Miss Ellsler's maple, a fine, large tree, is near the Mantell sun dial.

Near Juliet's flower bed is a tall elm planted by Jane Cowl during her second engagement in Cleveland for a portrayal of the unhappy daughter of the proud Capulets. Judge Willis Vickery, Shakespeare student and collector of Shakespeareana, delivered an address on this occasion.

It was under the auspices of the Federation of Women's Clubs education committee that many of the tree planting exercises were held as annual functions. Two Cleveland poets, Edmund Vance Cooke and Edwin Meade Robinson, are among those who have been honored in this manner. Carl T. Robertson, writer on nature themes, has also planted a tree in the Garden.

Belasco at Shakespeare Bust

Looking Across the Garden from Juliet's Rose Bed to Mantell Sun Dial

Many visiting Cleveland in winter and rough weather paid tribute to the bard by filling urns with vines and flowers for the Garden, while in the more comfortable confines of hotel quarters or during appearances at theaters. Mme. Sarah Bernhardt performed this ceremony upon the stage of a Cleveland play-house, but her urn with its ivy and roses, as well as those of Rabindranath Tagore, "The Shakespeare of India," and Sir Herbert Tree, who planted English ivy while appearing in the city as Cardinal Wolsey in a revival of Shakespeare's "Henry VIII" at the Opera House, have long been missing. Bronze inscriptions upon the brick

Effie Ellsler Plants a Maple
W. R. Rose (left); City Forester Hyatt (Center)

pedestals upon either side of the bust still bear the names of Tree and Tagore.

Mme. Bernhardt made her contribution to the Garden during one of her last appearances in the city. The event took place at the Opera House. The curtain had been lowered and when it was raised again the famous actress was borne to the stage to perform the planting ceremony. After a few words, Mme. Bernhardt placed the ivy and roses from the tomb of Juliet in the urn that stood before her. Floyd E. Waite, secretary of the Department of Public Service, in a brief address, expressed the city's appreciation.

Sir Herbert Tree planted his ivy in the urn, later set out in the Shakespeare Garden, while standing amid a throng of lords and ladies of the day of Bluff King Hal. Robert Mantell made his presentation of the dial during his appearance in "Macbeth" at the Colonial Theater. The acceptance address was made by Mr. Waite in the name of the city.

Succeeding administrations have steadily enlarged and improved the Shakespeare area and the cultural influence of its presence has expanded immeasurably with the passing years.

For Shakespeare's Garden is not successfully circummured. Its overrun is as far flung as the human yearning for beauty. Singing of his Garden Shakespeare puts a girdle round about the earth in one swift, poignant, searching phrase.

Life itself and all humanity are charted in his garden ken of stocks, slips, bud, bark and seed.

Hedgerows cast their deep shadows athwart his Italy, his France and his haunted Athenian domain. Avon murmurs by. But England's sea wall has not confined his restless vision.

Hovering low by ivy mantled cot; now skirting the greenest meadows; now soaring to the highest battlements; now mounting to heaven's gate on the wings of the lark, but not too far to note the buzzing of Ariel's bees and the glint of dew on every nodding chalice, the master poet's fancy ranges in most dazzling

Tagore Plants Ivy for Garden   flights at the beck and whisper of some flower comrade under the open sky. Shakespeare as gardener sings the loftiest strain.

THE BRUOT GATEWAY

RIGINALLY confined to the upper portion of the hill-side, the Garden may now be entered from the lower Boulevard through an English gateway erected in 1925 as a memorial tribute to the late Marie Leah Bruot, for more than thirty years teacher of English speech at Central High School, Cleveland.

The Shakespeare Club, a dramatic organization to which she devoted years of unabating enthusiasm, produced most of the plays of the poet at Central High School. Under Miss Bruot's inspiration, year by year many hundreds of students became fired with a devotion to the works of the Bard, that never departed from them in after-school years.

A memorial committee headed by George H. Barber was organized after her death in 1924. Because her life task had been the instilling of an abiding love for the beauties of Shakespeare into the boys and girls of her class, it was deemed fitting that her name be linked with the Shakespeare Garden in a memorial tribute. City Manager William R. Hopkins co-operated actively in the project and also gave immediate support to a proposal then made that the Gateway serve jointly as entrance to

Bruot Gate Inscription

Marie Leah Bruot

the Garden and to a small pastoral theater to be set in the hollow hard by.

A committee was named by the City Manager to consider plans for this development.

As a memorial to Miss Bruot a gate of stone and iron was designed by City Architect Herman Kregelius.   Upon each post was placed a tablet telling of Miss Bruot's service.

"For thousands of boys and girls Marie Leah Bruot was the gateway to the stately beauty of Shakespeare's matchless verse," reads the inscription upon the southerly tablet.

On September 5, 1925, the Bruot Memorial entrance gate was dedicated.   City and school officials participated in the event.   An orchestra rendered a program of Shakespeare music, including the "Midsummer Night's Dream Overture" of Mendelssohn, and Perdita's greeting was heard once more.   On this occasion the reader was Miss Virginia Whitworth.   The memorial presentation was made by George H. Barber.   An address was delivered by William R. Rose.   Park Director Frank S. Harmon accepted the gate in the name of the city.

"Midsummer Night's Dream" at the Shakespeare Garden Theater

THE SHAKESPEARE GARDEN THEATER

HORTLY after the completion of the Bruot Memorial, ground was broken for the small outdoor theater designed for use in productions of "As You Like It," "Midsummer Night's Dream" and other works which lend themselves to woodland and garden backgrounds.

The project had been under consideration for several years but definite progress was not made until it was decided that it should proceed with the construction of the Bruot Memorial entrance, the whole to form a definite and integral part of the Garden scheme, through the construction of a stairway uniting the lower and upper parts of the development. Knowledge that the theater was to be expressly designed for presentations of an intimate nature and that pageants and large musical productions were to be conducted in a great ampitheater, apart from the Garden, simplified the problem of determining upon a location.

The site selected was the wooded hillside just west of the Garden proper. A natural enclosure or hollow between two steep slopes leading from the upper Boulevard to the lower Boulevard driveway formed a secluded auditorium, but the location of the stage required considerable attention because it opened directly upon the latter drive. An apron stage was constructed by placing generous fills of earth in the lowest portion of the hollow. The auditorium slope required but little artificial aid in the way of grading, mounding or excavating.

The sylvan theater at the Washington Monument in the Capital served as the inspiration for its general construction. Park Commissioner Samuel Newman and City Forester Arthur L. Munson were active in this undertaking.

Ethel Barrymore Planting the Barrymore Hawthorn

In the spring of 1926, American hawthorn bushes were set out as a background and as wings. As a dedicatory planting event, Ethel Barrymore, then fresh from her triumphs as Ophelia and Portia, with Walter Hampden in New York productions of "Hamlet" and "The Merchant of Venice," was invited to place the first shovelfuls of earth about the roots of the "key" hawthorn, which conceals the stage exit in the hedge facing the hillside auditorium. City officials and representatives of Western Reserve University, then preparing for a Shakespeare production which was to mark the formal opening of the theater, took part in the program linked with the final planting for the stage.

City Manager Hopkins, who is the brother of Arthur Hopkins, famous theatrical producer and manager of John Barrymore in the days when the son of the late Maurice Barrymore and Georgia Drew Barrymore burst upon the theatrical horizon with his impersonation of Hamlet, referred in his address to the fame of the theatrical family of which Miss Barrymore is a member.

About a hundred years before the day that Miss Barrymore participated in the Shakespeare Garden Theater event, her grandmother, Mrs. John Drew, then the child-actress, Louisa Lane, made her debut in America at the Walnut Street Theater as the Duke of York in "Richard III." Nearly fifty years before the Shakespeare Garden Theater dedication, Maurice Barrymore, then newly arrived from England, was leading a Daly's Fifth Avenue Theater comedy production, at the Opera House in Cleveland.

Inspecting the Shakespeare Garden after the formal ceremony on the outdoor stage, Miss Barrymore showed keenest interest in the flowers of Shakespeare. Of rosemary,

Ethel Barrymore

pansies, fennel, there was none, and the summer days of columbine were yet to be. But poor Ophelia's violets, not withered, but fresh and fragrant in the sunlight of May, were growing in profusion along the pathways and sheltered portions of the yew-bordered beds.

Formal dedication of the Shakespeare Garden Theater took place on the evenings of June 15 and 16, with the presentation of "A Midsummer Night's Dream," a work which has not been featured with marked regularity by professional companies since the era of Daly, and has become more generally identified with the woodland or pastoral stage.

Ethel Barrymore and City Manager W. R. Hopkins Entering the Shakespeare Garden

Two Western Reserve University organizations, namely, the Sock and Buskin Club and the Curtain Players of the College for Women joined in the presentation which was arranged as a feature of the University's centennial celebration program.

But few of the stock stage traditions were followed in the production and yet, perhaps, it came as close to Elizabethan stage tradition as any performance in this age could profitably venture.

There were two notable departures. The

"—a Knavery of Them to Make Me Afeard"

costuming was historically accurate and the most modern of electrical lighting effects were used.

As settings, the distant panorama of trees, the hawthorn hedges in the foreground and a central platform with a series of steps giving the necessary classical touch to the Theseus palace scenes, were historically adequate in every sense of the word.

On the second night a real moon peered down with some curiosity upon his jovial counterpart equipped with lanthorn, thornbush and dog.

There was startling convincingness in the scene which Peter Quince, as impresario, embraced in one swift gesture as his fellow

Athenian amateur tragedians gathered in the haunted woods:

Pat, pat; and here's a marvelous convenient place for our rehearsal. This green plot shall be our stage, this hawthorne-brake our tiring house"—

There was truth in the starlight by which the gentle Thisbe timidly ventured forth to find her lover. There was joyous youth in the zest of the dainty Puck who bounded from bush to bush; in the impetuous wooing and impetuous quarreling of the harrassed lovers and in the romping of the fairy band.

"A Midsummer Night's Dream" is a comedy of youth. Youth officered and armied this cast.

It was Hazlitt who wrote many years ago that "the reader of the plays of Shakespeare is almost always disappointed in seeing them acted."

Because of the gossamer-like quality of its poetry, the shimmering beauty of its imagery, its shadowy shifting from real to unreal, "A Midsummer Night's Dream," as a stage production, does present practical difficulties that prove perplexing to the most seasoned stage craftsman.

But how many of these survive when the stage is a grass plot, shadowed by trees; fringed by hawthorn and when, brooding over all, gleams a mildly inquisitive moon?

Petty doubts and perplexities vanish. Elements that remain are those ingredients which deepen the spell of a master stage technician's masterly art.

Elbow room is here a plenty for the fine frenzy "that seeks the infinite to body forth the forms of things unknown,

> *Turns them to shapes, and gives to airy nothing*
> *A local habitation and a name."*

BIALIK

HAIM NACHMAN BIALIK, acclaimed by Hebraists as the greatest Hebrew poet since the days of Jehudah Halevi, as guest of honor in Cleveland May 5, 1926, visited the Poets' Corner and planted three Cedars of Lebanon.

The poet had come from Palestine for a tour of the country in behalf of the cause of Zion's restoration. At meetings arranged in his honor in many cities, thousands were stirred by his eloquent appeal.

A wooded tract near the Shakespeare Garden, selected for the planting, was to be reserved, it was then announced, for tributes to Hebrew poets.

Many admirers of the great poet gathered at the site despite a steady fall of rain, to honor the man whose modern-day message has been conveyed in the Hebrew of the Prophets of Israel.

City Manager William R. Hopkins, in his greeting, spoke of the contribution of Hebrew writers to the cultural advancement of the world. Rabbi Solomon Goldman, who presided at the tree planting exercises, translated the Hebrew address of the poet, and other participants in the program were Edmund Vance Cooke, Councilman A. R. Hatton and A. H. Friedland.

In his address the Hebrew poet, who is the author of a Hebrew translation of Shakespeare's "Julius Caesar," stressed the fact that the proposed Hebrew Poets' Corner faced the Shakespeare Garden and voiced the hope that in days to come the Cedars of Lebanon as tall and mighty trees would flourish as symbols of the culture

"Come Now; What Masques, What Dances Shall We Have?"

Bialik, Rabbi Goldman and City Manager Hopkins

that had its root in far off Palestine. Wherever there is a literary sense, Shakespeare and the Hebrew Bible share alike, the noted poet declared.

"The greatness of a poet is measured by his poems," said Mr. Cooke in his tribute. "The greatness of Chaim Nachman Bialik is measured by the love his people bear him. Chaim Nachman Bailik comes from a race of poets, poets who have sung their faith into their songs, and who have prophesied in proverbs and psalms and parables.

"Today he plants the older poetry into a newer earth, just as these Cedars of Lebanon representing his ancient faith of Palestine, yet are planted and take root in this new continent, this new commercial country, these newer vital surroundings. The Cedars of Lebanon are so vital they may almost be said to be immortal, and if they are not immortal in material reality, they are immortal in a truer sense; they are immortal in song and story. What makes them immortal? The symbolism of their evergreen fragrance representing an ancient faith. In other words, their poetry, for poetry is the most immortal thing in the world, if we can consider that there are degrees of immortality.

"If I were not afraid of precipitating a theological discussion among the faiths and unfaiths represented here this morning, I might say that immortality itself is poetry, inasmuch as it is that ideality we long for, but can only partially picture or comprehend. So, today, we have Chaim Nachman Bialik, representing an immortal race and faith, planting these Cedars of Lebanon, representing the immortal longing of a man for a sweeter, more fragrant, unfading existence, in memory of an immortal poet. And the significance of it all is that this ceremony occurs not in hoary Palestine, or in dreamy Stratford-on-Avon, but in this modern, throbbing, vital city of Cleveland, unsurpassed in its modernity by any city in the world."

While Chaim Nachman Bialik was a guest in Cleveland his plea was being sent throughout the land to Jewish children of America to aid in a movement to reforest the barren tracts of Palestine, bringing again, thereby, the glory of her youth:

"The birds also and all the myriads of winged songsters will return and fill the forests and the valleys with their singing. Let the trees rustle on the summits of her mountains, on the slopes of her valleys; let them fringe the roads and give shade by day to the wanderer and shelter and refreshment to the tired laborer."

BACKGROUNDS

A PASSING century's changing moods, as reflected in the wide sweep of literature, music and the drama, had left their impress upon the Forest City in the year in which the Shakspeare Garden and its neighboring tributes came into being.

Wilderness was still unconquered in the region of the Cuyahoga when the citizens of Cleveland gathered at early candle-light in Mowry's Hall at Superior street and the Public Square to witness the first theatrical performance within the confines of what is now Ohio's metropolis.

Wolves were howling along the westerly edges of the county. Deer, wild turkey and bear were to be had for the hunting.

That the first performance, a variegated affair, including a comic opera entitled "The Purse Won the Benevolent Tar," a drama entitled "The Strangers," a farce and specialty acts of singing and dancing, was a success is indicated by the prolonged stay of the visiting players. Bearing out this assumption is a farewell announcement in the Cleaveland Herald of May 30, 1820, just seven days after the opening presentation. This is to the effect that at Mowry's Hall, Cleaveland—being positively the last night— Mr. Blanchard, feeling himself indebted to the citizens of Cleaveland for their kind and liberal reception of his endeavors to please, returns to them his sincere thanks and also begs leave to inform them that he will offer, for their satisfaction and amusement, on Wednesday evening, May 31, the entire play of "The Mountaineers" with songs, duets, etc., etc.

A farce entitled "The Village Lawyer" was the light touch of the farewell evening's endeavors. "Blue Eyed Mary," a duet was sung by Mr. and Miss Blanchard.

In 1893, the late Maurice Weidenthal, in a history of the theater in Cleveland written for the Amusement Gazette, commented as follows upon the Blanchard engagement in Cleaveland Village:

"Julia B. Blanchard was the leading lady. She was the manager's daughter, and when the troupe departed on the lake, taking the sail-vessel 'Tiger,' she left many a broken heart behind among the young fellows in the town and among the youthful farmers, who walked in and walked home many miles, through fields and forest. Subsequently Miss Blanchard married a United States officer stationed at Fort Mackinac."

In 1831 Cleveland first beheld Shakespeare enstaged. Phinney Mowry's tavern auditorium had yielded to the larger communal needs. The newer town gathering place was the belfried court house of Georgian architecture which adorned the southwest section of the Public Square.

In that period, Junius Brutus Booth and Edwin Forrest, still in early manhood years, were beginning to garner fame and glory. Two years were to elapse before the last scene of all for Edmund Kean. But for stately Sarah Siddons, Tragic Muse of Joshua Reynold's immortal canvas and fellow performer, earlier in her career, with the great Davy Garrick himself, it was the year of the final call.

In that same eventful period, a tiny black-eyed maiden of ten, one day to be known as Rachel, the world's greatest tragedienne, was singing "The Marseillaise" in the streets of Paris.

Remote as yet from the paths of these mighty ones, the tiny frontier village still set in the heart of primeval woodlands, enjoyed the Shakespearean presentations of Gilbert & Trowbridge with Mrs. Trowbridge as female lead.

But a few years more and Cleveland, stimulated to a rapid rate of progress by the newly completed canal, began to boast of its Apollo Hall, where the elder Booth and Forrest and other renowned figures began to appear.

A Near View of the Bust and Lily Pool

And when young Charles Dickens, in the course of his American Travels, in the year 1842, happened upon Cleveland of an April morning, the town that lay before him as he strolled along Superior avenue boasted several book stores, literary and debating societies and at least four fine auditoriums.

The Globe, ordained to play a prominent part throughout forty years of Cleveland's history, shone then in its pristine splendor.   Before its passing it was destined to echo to the bird message of Adelina Patti's youthful vocal flights.   Critics of Cleveland who had heard Jenny Lind in all her glory but four years before, on the occasion of her memorable recital at Kelley's Hall, predicted a brilliant future for the newer star in the concert firmament.

To the Globe (it was then known as Melodeon Hall) came Emerson, who on one visit did not escape the rollicking condemnation of Artemus Ward, then associate editor of the Plain Dealer, for attempting, even temporarily, to depart from his well suited role of purveyor of the written word for that of orator. But Artemus himself, it might be noted, in later years, did not overlook an opportunity to appear in the same hall as lecturer, though in a far less ponderous vein.

Old Academy of Music on Bank Street

At the Globe, appeared Laura Keene, brilliant actress of the mid-nineteenth century, whose "Our American Cousin" was the production at Ford's Theater in Washington on the night of President Lincoln's assassination.   On December 2, 1859, Melodeon Hall was the scene of a mass meeting of Cleveland's citizenry "to give expression to public sentiment on the occasion of the sacrifice to the Moloch of Slavery by the killing of John Brown by the commonwealth of Virginia." The meeting revealed the feeling aroused by John Brown's execution.

Most fittingly, because of that historic association, the final performance at the old auditorium was "Uncle Tom's Cabin" ever a favorite, both as novel and play, in a city which from its earliest history had been keenly anti-slavery. Years before the Globe's farewell endeavor, Harriet Beecher Stowe appeared before a Cleveland audience, and gave a reading from her famous epic.

As temple of the dramatic arts, the Globe's beacon did not gleam with the steady flare of Cleveland's "Old Drury," the Academy of Music, which began its remarkable career in 1852 and reached its zenith under the directing genius of John A. Ellsler, renowned character actor, producer and manager.

John A. Ellsler

It was the era of the stock company, disciplined to meet on short notice the repertoire demands of such traveling stars as Forrest, Davenport, Fechter, the Booths, Charlotte Cushman and others of e q u a l attainment. Trained as well to match exacting talent from without, with talent from within.

From John Ellsler's school, like that of Impresario William Shakespeare, a living stage in actual use before very live assemblages, arose such personalities as Clara Morris (who passed away in 1925 at the age of seventy-six, following many decades of suffering caused by a lingering illness), and Effie Ellsler, daughter of John, two of the remarkably gifted emotional actresses of the age.

Joseph Haworth, hailed at the height of his strength as the heir to the princely mantle of Edwin Booth's melancholy Dane,

obtained a knowledge of dramatic expression under the same
tutelage.

Shakespeare was a foundation stone in the Ellsler training.
Behind the Cora, the "New Magdalen," the Renee de Moray
and the Camille of Clara Morris at the sweep of her emotional
heights in the 70's or 80's lay the patient mounting of the ladder
by minor Shakespeare
roles in "Old Drury" of
Bank street in Cleveland,
where she had studied the
methods of earlier stars,
the Booths and the Cush-
mans and humbly bided
the call of her own great
opportunity.

Unvanquished by a
first disappointment at
her Shakespeare debut,
namely, her assignment
to the role of page to
Paris instead of page to
Romeo, with its fatter
speaking opportunities,
the saucer-eyed, apple
cheeked girl who aroused
Edwin Booth's half jest-
ing demurrer when he learned she had been selected to play the
Queen Mother to his Hamlet, made the greatest of Emilias in
"Othello" and won the whole-hearted admiration of many
theatergoers in after times for the originality of her conception of
Lady Macbeth, opposed in every detail to the masculine portrayal
favored by the prevailing school.

Behind the Bessie Barton and Hazel of Effie Ellsler, whose
emotional power wrung the hearts of countless thousands in
triumphal tours of the nation in "Woman Against Woman" and
"Hazel Kirk" long after the Academy days had ceased to be, was
her childhood-day Virginia to the Virginius of Edwin Forrest, in

Clara Morris

his last farewell.   For him, night's candle had burned low and the Academy program footnote writer believed it to be delicately in keeping to stress the glorious yesteryear of Forrest's art in condonation of the fast falling darkness.

But in that year of 1872, when Forrest had closed his eyes in death, critics referred to the exquisite tenderness of the Virginius of his last farewell.

Effie Ellsler, at thirteen, was called from school to be the Virginia to that Virginius.   Then followed the days of Juliet, of Rosalind, of Fanchon, Oliver Twist (with Mrs. Effie Ellsler as Nancy), of Arline, of Zoe the Octoroon, of Bartley Campbell's "Heroine in Rags" and a host of other creations of the shadow world of that and far earlier generations.

Effie Ellsler

Though the passing of the Academy approaches with the rise of the Opera House erected on old Sheriff street at Euclid avenue by John Ellsler in the year 1875, there is no immediate break in tradition.   The old names endure. Young Haworth is advanced to more important roles.   He is Orlando to Effie Ellsler's Rosalind. His name appears with the visiting stars, but more than a decade was to elapse before his great Boston triumph in "Hamlet," bringing full realization to the prediction of Edwin Booth, who in Hamlet garb had studied the Haworth Laertes from the wings and had read in his youthful strivings the first expressions of mounting genius.

The day was changing.   In that Centennial period in Cleveland the stock and traveling star systems were yielding to the traveling star and traveling company with vast scenic equipment and an array of the property detail that is anathema in modernist dramatic art circles of the day.

With Irving and Terry, whom Cleveland in 1884 beheld for the first time, in productions of "Louis XI," "Merchant of Venice" and "Much Ado About Nothing," scenic lavishness reached the newer heights. Shakespeare as presented by many American stars of the Irving-Terry period shone forth in the same splendid accoutrement. But all of this did not submerge the glory of the Irving-Terry art, and a decade which witnessed the co-star presentations of Booth and Barrett, the triumphal tour of Mary Anderson and of Salvini, mightiest of all Othellos, and Modjeska and the stellar debuts of Marlowe and Sothern, need never clamor for the services of a champion or apologist.

Booth and Barrett's first joint appearance in Cleveland took place at the Opera House in a production of "Julius Caesar" on November 14, 1887. Of that event Maurice Weidenthal, as theatrical critic of the Plain Dealer, wrote:

"It was apparently an expectant and impatient audience, for the opening scenes of the tragedy passed by almost unnoticed, all eyes being strained to catch a glimpse of the two stars. When they finally did appear together there was a momentary hush and then a burst of greeting, in whose spontaneity any actor might have taken just pride. The two stars slowly descended the stairway, they appeared before the footlights, the action of the play was resumed and the audience, only a moment before wildly enthusiastic, settled down to be coldly critical."

It was from Cleveland, on April 17, 1889, that Edwin Booth, stricken with a slight stroke of paralysis but two weeks before in Rochester, wrote a letter to his daughter, Mrs. Edwina Booth Grossman, in answer to her anxious inquiries, assuring her that Barrett was doing all that could be done to lighten the task of completing the season. All of the one-night engagements had been cancelled, he informed Mrs. Grossman, and in his letter he repeatedly emphasized the point that despite the assertions of anxious friends, he was not being overworked and that his manager was doing all that could possibly be done to prevent his strength from being overtaxed. The fact that his appearance under contract had its business phase that could not be overlooked was also dealt with in his letter.

Edwin Booth gave his last performance of Hamlet two years later in New York. His death occurred in 1893. Poor Barrett, also in failing health when the Cleveland engagement was being filled in 1889, preceded Booth to the final rest. He had been a frequent visitor at the Opera House and in earlier years was a featured player at the Academy.

The Booth performance in Cleveland in 1889 was praised by Cleveland critics as bearing the full impress of his early powers, though William Winter maintains in his Booth biography that his decline was apparent after the Rochester breakdown. In the fall of that same year, Booth returned to Cleveland with Mme. Helena Modjeska as co-star in a repertoire consisting of "Richelieu," "Much Ado About Nothing," "Donna Diana" and "The Fool's Revenge." Otis Skinner was a member of the Booth-Modjeska supporting cast.

The Salvinis, father and son, appeared in Cleveland, at first, jointly. Young Alexander was given his first opportunity by Clara Morris. He was the Romeo to Margaret Mather's Juliet and later he played repeatedly in Cleveland in a repertoire of romantic roles, including the perennially youthful D'Artagnan and Don Caesar de Bazan. It was at the Stillman Hotel in Cleveland that Maude Dixon, well-known American actress who led the Salvini supporting cast, became the bride of the young Italian. Death came to the brilliant young actor in the year 1896, when he was in the height of his artistic strength and popularity. Salvini the elder followed him in 1916.

Father and son are now at rest in San Miniato, in beautiful Florence.

Julia Marlowe made her debut in Cleveland as Parthenia in the now well-nigh forgotten "Ingomar." To Miss Marlowe fate had granted the rare privilege denied the youthful Clara Morris twenty years before at the old Academy, inasmuch as her first Shakespeare appearance had been as Romeo's page in all the glory of red and black velvet.

This impression of the art of the girl of twenty who first appeared in Cleveland March 5, 1888, at the Park Theater on the

Public Square, is from the pen of the late Maurice Weidenthal, then dramatic critic of the Plain Dealer:

"Miss Marlowe rather surprised those who expected to see an amateur, a young beginner who does not know her place and one who wants to push ahead of her stirring and ambitious sisters of the stage without the necessary preliminary practical experience. True, she lacks some of the elements that help to make a successful whole, but it will not take many seasons ere she will master all these requirements, for she has the true fire and genius of an actress and she will make herself heard with no uncertain sound, and not at a distant day, either"

An "Academy" Program of November 8, 1873

But a few weeks before Miss Marlowe's initial bow to a Cleveland audience, E. H. Sothern played for the first time in the Forest City, in a stellar capacity. His vehicle was "The Highest Bidder." The heading of a local critique following the opening night of the engagement read: "Sothern's son at the Opera House." The memory of E. A. Sothern was then fresh and glowing. The beloved creator of droll Lord

Dundreary had appeared in Cleveland for the last time, in the dawn of the '80's. Sothern passed away in 1881.

Before its demolition, in the second decade of the new century, the Opera House beheld the triumph of Mansfield with his Shakespearean ventures of Richard III, Brutus and Shylock, following his earlier successes in more modern portrayals.

But Shakespeare as steady fare was no more. The Bard was slowly passing into the hands of an ever dwindling group of players, and when John Ellsler, at seventy-five, was tenderly led by young Orlando to the stage of the Opera House to play Adam to the Rosalind of his daughter, in the sunset of a life extending well through the span of the nineteenth century, his was the vantage point for the survey of a proud and glittering epoch.

Edmund Kean, Rachel, the Kembles, Macready, Forrest, the Booths, Barrett, Mc Cullough, Bernhardt, Charlotte Cushman, Davenport, Fechter, Irving, Sonnenthal, Ristori, Duse—all had trod the boards within that span.

In the years of his century, Adelaide Neilson, queen-rose of the rosebud garland of Juliets, had shone in radiance, and all too quickly passed away.

O Proserpina!   For the flowers now—

But loyalties to vanished springtimes cannot arrest the panorama of the shifting years. Out of old forms arise the new.

Proserpina's blossoms live only in succession.

Were they but painted images, in the Poets' Corner of the vast domain of human accomplishment, who would put the dibble in earth to set one slip of them?

NOTES

Plan of Shakespeare Garden

A. Sothern Elm
B. Marlowe Elm
C. Mantell Sun Dial
D. Juliet's Roses
E. Shakespeare Bust
F. Faversham Willow
G. Frohman Willow
H. Shakespeare Mulberry
I. Ellsler Maple
J. Birnam Wood

PAGE 19

City Forester John Boddy's first public announcement of the plan for the establishment of a Shakespeare Garden followed prolonged and careful preliminary study and effort in assembling many of the English garden flowers which the poet loved. The garden was laid out during the mayoralty term of Harry L. Davis and while Alex Bernstein was the city's director of parks and public service. Floyd E. Waite and Harry C. Hyatt, as park director and city forester, respectively, in later years continued the work begun in 1916. Under the general administration of City Manager William R. Hopkins and the park directorship of Frank S. Harmon, with Arthur L. Munson as city forester, a number of features were added, including a rock garden, serving as background for the bust, the setting out of Birnam Grove and the extension of the garden area to the Bruot Gateway and theater. Raymond F. Persche, succeeding Mr. Munson as city forester, continued the development of the outdoor theater begun under the active direction of Park Commissioner Samuel Newman and Mr. Munson. Councilman J. E. Smith was one of the earliest supporters of the garden project and served as chairman of the Council Committee that directed the tercentenary event. Glenville High School gave the movement active backing.

Shakespeare's flower favorite, if frequent references in his works may be taken as the test, is by all odds the rose. The queen of flowers is mentioned by him in no less than sixty-five distinct passages in his works, not including the Temple Garden scene in King Henry VI. The lily is named in twenty-eight passages in his works. The violet, primrose, marigold, daisy, flower-de-luce, pansy or love-in-idleness, cowslip and daffodil are also among those repeatedly and lovingly named by the Bard. Honeysuckle and wild thyme are also favorites.

Eglantine and sweet brier in Shakespeare's time were terms used interchangeably. The fragrance of the eglantine is noted by all visitors at the Cleveland Garden.

"Thou shalt not lack
The flower that's like thy face, pale primrose, nor
The azur'd hare-bell, like thy veins, no, nor
The leaf of eglantine, whom not to slander,
Out-sweeten'd not thy breath"—

croons Arviragus in Shakespeare's "Cymbeline" to the sleeping Fidele.

PAGE 21

The Tomb of the Capulets at Verona is the first objective of the thousands of tourists who visit Verona annually. Despite the cold water which scholarly erudition has persistently thrown upon Luigi de Porto's story which has served as the inspiration of Shakespeare's beautiful tragedy of "Romeo and Juliet," the tradition lives on with rugged endurance. The tomb is in a chapel in the ancient Capuchin cemetery overlooking the Adige river. At the request of Dr. Nicola Cerri, former Italian Vice Consul at Cleveland, the Mayor of Verona, in 1916, forwarded vines and roses from the tomb, for planting in the Cleveland Garden. The vines have long since ceased to be, but the frail Italian roses or their little descendants are carefully placed in the Gordon Park greenhouse each year with the oncome of the northern winter days, and restored to their place in the Garden each year with the advent of summer.

PAGE 22

The Garden Bust Dedication of Oct. 21, 1916, followed the organization of a Shakespeare Memorial Committee under the chairmanship of W. J. Raddatz, president of the Cleveland Advertising Club. Serving as members with Mr. Radditz were: Floyd E. Waite, Secretary

to the Director of Public Service:
Mavor Harry L. Davis; Public Service Director Alex Bernstein; J. M.
H. Frederick, Superintendent of
Public Schools; Richard H. Lee,
president of the Cleveland Automo-
bile Club; J. M. Telleen, president
of the Drama League; A. R. Hatton,
president of the City Club; C. P. P.
Vitz, vice librarian, Public Library;
N. A. Collins, director of Young
Men's Business Club; Leo Weiden-
thal, of the Cleveland Plain Dealer;
S. S. Wilson, president of the An-
drews Institute for Girls (now sec-
retary and treasurer of Western
Reserve University); Judge Willis
Vickery; E. E. Admire, Cleveland
Chamber of Industry; Rt. Rev. T. C.
O'Reilly, D. D.

Sir Sidney Lee died in London on
March 3, 1926, at the age of sixty-
six. It was his hope in his declin-
ing years that his remains would
be interred close to those of Shakespeare. A few days after his death,
the Stratford Memorial Theater
was burned to the ground. His gift
to the city of Cleveland in 1916
came to City Forester John Boddy,
after a letter had been received
from another Stratford Memorial
official denying the city's request
for seeds or cuttings from plants
in the garden of the Anne Hathaway cottage at Shottery. A letter
from Sir Sidney Lee followed this
missive, explaining that the mulberry cutting was on its way.

The Shakespeare Mulberry was
grown from one of the slips distrib-
uted throughout England by M.
Francois Veron, a Frenchman, com-
missioned by King James I to aid
in this manner in the introduction
of silk worm culture into England. From Veron, Shakespeare,
then dwelling at New Place, received
some of the slips. In the eighteenth
century the famous mulberry tree
was cut down by Rev. Francis Gas-
trell, who had purchased the property and did not desire to be dis-
turbed by the tourists brought by
his fellow townsmen to his study
window to see the Shakespeare

memento. King James' effort to in-
troduce the silk industry went for
nought, as the mulberry slips, it
seems, were not of the white mulberry stock, the kind that the silk
worm demands. The entomological
faux pas of King James (or was
it perhaps that of M. Veron?) is
brought rather painfully to mind by
the following paragraph that appears
in the Nature Calendar of the Cleveland Museum of Natural History,
dated July 24, 1926: "Mulberries are
ripe. In the Shakespeare Garden
there are half a dozen berries form-
ing on the Birth-place tree (a black
mulberry)." The black mulberry is
of Persian origin and Shakespeare
viewing the tree in his New Place
garden, doubtlessly, was far less in-
terested in the issue of silk worm
dietetics than in the fact that this
was the tree that played a part in
the lives of Pyramus and Thisbe.

PAGE 23

The inaugural planting ceremony
of April 14, 1916, was marked by
the following program: Overture,
Walter's Orchestra; Introduction,
Floyd E. Waite, Secretary Depart-
ment of Public Service; Address,
Harry L. Davis, Mayor of Cleveland;
Selections, Normal School Glee
Club—"Hark! Hark; the Lark,"
"Who Is Sylvia?" Director, Mrs.
Harriet Parsons; Address, E. H.
Sothern; Selection, Midsummer
Night's Dream, Orchestra; Reading,
Flower Scene from "Winter's Tale,"
Julia Marlowe; Planting Exercises,
Miss Marlowe and Mr. Sothern.
Direction, John Boddy, City For-
ester. The exercises took place
from a speakers' stand erected on
the west side of the roadway and
directly opposite the entrance to the
Garden. Mr. Sothern's assigned part
in the event was a reading, but he
gave an informal talk instead, in
which he urged that the city institute story telling days for children
in the public parks. On the evening
of the day set aside for the Shakespeare Garden planting ceremony,
Alfred Noyes, famous English poet,

was a speaker at the Hotel Statler ballroom in Cleveland.

PAGE 28

Phyllis Neilson Terry, daughter of Fred Terry and Julia Neilson and niece of Ellen Terry, made her first appearance as Juliet in London in September, 1911. Two years later she appeared as Viola in Sir Herbert Tree's revival of "Twelfth Night."

PAGE 29

David Belasco's visit at the Shakespeare Garden occured some years prior to his most ambitious Shakespeare effort, namely, the elaborate production of "The Merchant of Venice," with David Warfield as Shylock. His planting of the junipers was a ceremony reverently performed, although no formal program had been arranged. The noted playwright and producer showed keen interest in the Garden. In reminiscences of his early San Francisco days, Belasco has noted that by way of practical Shakespeare experience, as a boy, he was assigned by Barry Sullivan to all the flying messenger roles in the Sullivan Shakespearean reportoire.

PAGE 33

Effie Ellsler was appearing in a Cleveland theatrical engagement when the city extended the invitation to participate in a tree planting ceremony at the Shakespeare Garden. A large gathering of Clevelanders, some of whom had been devoted admirers of her art from the early Academy of Music days, was on hand to welcome the creator of Hazel Kirk and Bessie Barton. Miss Ellsler's brothers, John J. Ellsler and Will C. Ellsler, were present at the planting ceremony.

Jane Cowl's first appearance in Cleveland in "Romeo and Juliet" preceded her opening in New York with this production. Her remarkable success in the Metropolis as the heroine of Shakespeare's love tragedy is a matter of theatrical history.

The Federation of Women's Clubs through its education committee has been in active touch with the Garden development from its earliest years. A plan to build an Anne Hathaway Cottage replica in the Garden, as a Memorial Museum, has enlisted the interest of the organization. Former City Forester Munscn addressed the Federation on this subject at a gathering and a committee was later named.

PAGE 37

Marie Leah Bruot was born in France, but came to America at the age of three. Her early years were spent in Akron, O., and she was graduated from Akron High School at seventeen. For three or four years she taught in the district schools of Summit County, Ohio. In the early '80's Miss Bruot left for Cleveland and for several years conducted a private school in English and oratory. After some years spent in study at the American Academy of Dramatic Art in New York City, as well as at the University of Geneva, Switzerland, Miss Bruot became teacher of English and oratory at West High School, from which position she was transferred shortly afterwards, to Central High School, where she remained head of the dramatic department until her resignation in 1921. For more than twenty-five years all of the better known works of Shakespeare were regularly produced under her direction. Miss Bruot was an ardent traveler. In November, 1923, she returned from a tour of the world. Included in her trip was a visit of some months in her native France. Miss Bruot's death occurred suddenly on April 30, 1924. The inscriptions upon the bronze plates of the Memorial Gate are as follows: "Gateway to Shakespeare Garden. Memorial Tribute to Marie Leah Bruot, 1857-1924, teacher of English Speech, Central High School, 1885-

1921. For thousands of boys and girls Marie Leah Bruot was the gateway to the stately beauty of Shakespeare's matchless verse."

The **Bruot Memorial Executive** Committee consisted of George H. Barber, Leo Weidenthal, Samuel Newman, Valerian Vlchek and Sartur Andrzejewski. The Advisory Committee consisted of Judge Willis Vickery, Mrs. Clara Tagg Brewer, William R. Rose, Miss Ruth Stone, William J. Raddatz, Miss Mary E. Adams and Archie Bell. In his letter to former pupils of Central High School, announcing that it had been proposed that the Bruot Memorial be linked with the Shakespeare Garden, Chairman Barber said: "In the opinion of Miss Bruot's friends, no more fitting tribute could be paid to one who has done so much to inculcate a true appreciation of the noblest in literature and the drama, than to perpetuate her name in this beautiful spot, dedicated as it is to the Master Poet, whose works she so dearly loved."

PAGE 39

The **Bruot Memorial Gateway** dedication, September 5, 1925, took place at the then still uncompleted Shakespeare Garden Theater. In addition to the addresses, there was a program of appropriate music by the Logan Concert Orchestra, including in addition to the Midsummer Night's Dream Overture, a fantasie based upon Gounod's "Romeo and Juliet" and German's Dances from Henry VIII. During Miss Whitworth's reading of the Flower Scene from "Winter's Tale," Mendelssohn's Midsummer Night's Dream Nocturne was played.

PAGE 41

"A Midsummer Night's Dream" was presented by the Western Reserve Sock and Buskin and Curtain Clubs on the occasion of the dedication of the Shakespeare Garden Theater, June 15 and 16, 1926, under the direction of K. Elmo Lowe of the Playhouse, and with Barclay S. Leathem as club director and Prof. H. S. Woodward as faculty advisor. The full cast of the production follows: Theseus, Allen Goldthwaite; Egeus, Sidney Markowitz; Lysander Ralph A. Colbert; Demetrius, Fred W. Walter; Philostrate, Richard Barker; Quince, John Maurer; Snug, Arlin Cook; Bottom, Milton Widder; Flute, Sterling S. Parker; Snout, Will Carlton; Straveling, Vincent H. Jenkins; Hippolyta, Doris Young; Hermia, Nadine Miles; Helena, Fredrica Crane; Oberon, Sidney Andorn; Titania, Eleanor Koob; Puck, Emiah Jane Hopkins; First Fairy. Katherine M. Squire; Peasblossom, Evelyn Fruehauf; Cobweb, Helen Shockley; Moth, Lucile McMackin; Mustardseed, Gladys M. Benesch; Court Ladies, Harriette Winch, Helen Bunnell; Gentlemen of the Court, Robert Glick, Maurice Rusoff, Titania's Train, Miriam Cramer, Fay Hart, Alice Sorensen, Caroline Hahn. Incidental music for the production was written by Quincy Porter of the Cleveland Institute of Music.

PAGE 43

Arthur Hopkins was given full and unstinted credit for his part in the shaping of the career of the most noted American Hamlet of the present age, at the opening Barrymore production of the tragedy in Cleveland at the Hanna Theater. In a characteristic curtain speech, Mr. Barrymore spoke in glowing terms of the producer who had been identified with all of his great stage successes.

PAGE 47

Chaim Nachman Bialik was born in a village of South Russia in the year 1873. His father was an innkeeper on the outskirts of the village. Following his father's death he was taken to live with his grandfather. An ardent student of Hebrew in his earliest youth, by thirteen he had thoroughly absorbed the works of the Hebraic sages and philosophers. At dawning manhood he came under the influence of Achad Ha'am, and Bialik's zeal for the cause of Zionism began under his teaching. Bialik wrote many of his earlier works while located at Odessa. In 1904 the poet first went to Palestine. For a number of years it has been his permanent home.

PAGE 52

Maurice Weidenthal began his career as a newspaper writer in 1876, acting in the capacity, as well, of Cleveland correspondent of the New York Dramatic News. In that service he formed his early acquaintance with theatrical affairs. In November, 1882, he received a call from the Cleveland Herald, where he became dramatic and musical critic. When the Plain Dealer succeeded to the plant of the Herald, he continued as dramatic editor and assistant city editor. Some years later he resigned to accept the post of city editor of the Sun. For a brief period he was contributor to Town Topics and had charge of the Sun and Voice. About six months after his resignation from the Plain Dealer he was called to the post of city editor for that publication, a position which he held until 1893, when he assumed charge of the theatrical departments of the World and the Amusement Gazette. Later he became political editor and theatrical critic for the Press. In 1906 he left the daily newspaper field to assume the editorship of the Jewish Independent, a publication founded at that time. His death occurred in 1917.

PAGE 54

The Globe was situated on the Superior avenue, N. W., site where the Wilshire Building was later erected. The latter structure was used as a temporary Post Office, while the present Federal Building was under construction.

PAGE 55

The Academy of Music was located in a structure on the east side of W. 6th street (old Bank street), between St. Clair and Frankfort avenues. The building (in 1926) is still standing. The first production in the old play-house was given in the early 50's of the past century.

John Adam Ellsler was born in Philadelphia, Sept. 26, 1822. In early youth he learned the trade of a confectioner, but deserted that occupation upon finding that it was injurious to his health. Through the assistance of a friend he secured a position as assistant treasurer of Peale's Museum at the munificent salary of $4 a week. In addition to performing the duties of assistant treasurer, for this wage he was expected to assume the responsibilities of candle-snuffer, supernumerary and property man as well. He first appeared as an actor in 1846. While he was most regularly assigned to comedy parts, it soon appeared that his forte as actor was old men's roles. His marriage to Mrs. Effie Meyers, a widow, took place during his first year upon the stage. Mrs. Ellsler was of a prominent theatrical family and was herself an actress of great ability. Of her first marriage there were two children, Harry and Fred. Both adopted the name of their step-father. To Mr. and Mrs. Ellsler, four children were born, Effie, Annie, John J. and Will C. After some time in Philadelphia and New York John Ellsler was called to a stock company in Charleston, S. C. It was here that he formed his life-long friendship with Joseph Jefferson, then a member of the company. Jefferson and Mrs. Jefferson later toured with the Ellslers. It is said that Jefferson obtained his grasp of the Dutch dialect he used as Rip Van Winkle under John Ellsler's fine schooling. It was in 1855 that John Ellsler assumed the management of the Academy of Music. One of the members of his first company was Mrs. G. H. Gilbert, who in later years attained nation-wide fame in character roles in Augustine Daly's company. Mrs. Gilbert, than newly arrived from England, was a danseuse in the early Academy days. In the same company was James Lewis, who later became comedian in the Daly organization. James O'Neill, father of Eugene O'Neill, was leading man of the company for a period. One of John Ellsler's notable successes as producer was "Aladdin," in which he appeared as Kazrac, a mute. He was also successful as Dogberry in "Much Ado About Nothing," Adam in "As You Like It," and similar roles.

Clara Morris appeared in her first speaking part at the old Academy on Nov. 20, 1863. Her role was the Spirit of Home in "Dot, or the Cricket on the Hearth." In that production Effie Ellsler, then a child of five, appeared as the Cricket. Five years after her first speaking part venture in "The Cricket," Clara Morris had so advanced in her art that a special benefit was arranged in her honor. The Cleveland Herald of June 26, 1868, makes this announcement of the occasion:

"This evening that charming young and talented actress, Clara Morris, calls upon her friends for a benefit. She has by her careful attention to her duties risen to a high position in her profession, and we expect to see the house packed. A splendid bill is to be presented, the new and original drama, "The Duel in the Mist,' will be presented for the first time in this city, and the laughable comedy, 'Our Hotel Bootblack,' will close the performance." According to then current reports, it was upon the recommendation of James Lewis, who as member of the Ellsler company had observed her work, that Clara Morris was called to the Daly Company in New York. Her first metropolitan appearance was in 1870. The play was "Man and Wife." Her first appearance in "Camille" was in 1874. In the same period she played in Shakespearean roles, for which her training in Cleveland had served in good stead.

In 1883 she appeared with Salvini. Illness forced her to retire some ten years later and her appearances in after times were merely occasional. In 1904 she returned to the stage as Sister Genevieve in an all-star benefit revival of "The Two Orphans." Her suffering became intense and for a period she was blind. In her autobiographical work" Life on the Stage," Clara Morris tells of her girlhood years in Cleveland and of her training at the Academy. A memorial exhibit at the Cleveland Publci Library after her death, on Nov. 21, 1925, displayed this extract from her work: "So many plays were produced, representing so many periods, so many countries, I don't know how I should have satisfied my craving for the books they led me to, had not the Public Library opened just then." The body of Clara Morris lay in state at the Little Church Around the Corner, in New York. The New York newspapers noted that in the same chapel had reposed the bodies of Richard Mansfield, Joseph Jefferson, Edwin Booth and Maurice Barrymore. It was Maurice Barrymore, a member of the Daly company in the period in which Clara Morris' genius was most dominating, who declared in a public interview many years after the Daly stock company days: "Actresses who really possess the divine afflatus are few and far between. Clara Morris is one of them. Eleanora Duse is another. One moment of inspiration is worth all the traditional acting in the world."

Joseph Haworth was born in Providence, but in his early years the family moved to Cleveland. His first determination to be an actor was formed when as a youngster he climbed to the gallery of the old Academy and witnessed from that lofty vantage ground a particularly thrilling production of "Monte Cristo." "Every detail of that first scene comes back to me as if I had seen it last night," he said many years later, when his Hamlet was regarded as a masterpiece of the day. "The harbor at Marseilles, the sailors, the sea and the clouds beyond. When the play was over, I said to my cousin: 'The best one on the stage was the little girl who played Mercedes.' That little girl was no other than Clara Morris, whose genius was evident even to my boyish judgment. Years afterwards I acted with her in "Denise" in New York, when she was considered by many critics to be the greatest actress on the American stage." Among Haworth's notable roles, besides his Hamlet, were Macbeth, Paul Kauvar in the play of that name, St. Marc, Richelieu and Richard III. With Modjeska he played Macbeth, Sir Edward Mortimer in "Mary Stuart," Claudio in "Measure for Measure" and many other roles. He supported McCullough and Mansfield and appeared as Romeo to the Juliet of Mary Anderson.

PAGE 58

Mary Anderson appeared in a notable series of productions in Cleveland at the Opera House in February, 1886. On that occasion J. Forbes Robertson, now Sir Johnston Forbes-Robertson, was her leading man. "Pygmalion and Galatea," "Comedy and Tragedy" (written for Miss Anderson by W. S. Gilbert) "Lady of Lyons" and "As You Like It" made up the repertoire. In the last named play, the Orlando was Sir Johnston-Forbes-Robertson. A cable from London on Feb. 24, 1926, published by American newspapers reported an address by the famous English actor on Feb. 23, before a stationers' convention, in which he recalled his experience on the stage as co-star or leading man with Ellen Terry, Adelaide Neilson, Mme. Modjeska, Mrs. Patrick Campbell, Mary Anderson and Gertrude Elliott.

PAGE 60

Richard Mansfield's earliest starring venture came, it is pointed out by William Winter in his Mansfield biography, when Kyrle Bellew, Maurice Barrymore, John Drew, J. H. Gilmore, Joseph Haworth and E. H. Sothern were all eminent figures in the theater. To this list Mr. Winter might well have added James O'Neill, then in the very zenith of his career as an actor of romantic and heroic roles. Mr. O'Neill was leading man at the Academy of Music in Cleveland during the John Ellsler stock company period. James O'Neill will ever be identified with the role of Edmund Dantes in "The Count of Monte Cristo," a play in which he toured the country for many seasons. An interesting sketch of the life of Eugene O'Neill, eminent playwright, written by David Karsner for the New York Herald-Tribune of Aug. 8, 1926, devotes considerable space to the life of the playwright's father, James O'Neill. Eugene O'Neill's mother, Mr. Karsner relates, first met James O'Neill while attending the convent school in Cleveland. Mr. and Mrs. O'Neill were married in 1877.

CPSIA information can be obtained
at www.ICGtesting.com
Printed in the USA
LVHW012137020820
662196LV00020B/2741